UNLOCKING
THE
MYSTERY
OF THE
BIBLE

STUDENT WORKBOOK

Jeff Cavins & Sarah Christmyer

ASCENSION PRESS

West Chester, Pennsylvania

Nihil obstat: Rev. Robert A. Pesarchick, S.T.D.
                  Censor Librorum
                  February 27, 2015

Imprimatur: +Most Reverend Charles J. Chaput, O.F.M. Cap.
                  Archbishop of Philadelphia
                  March 2, 2015

Unlocking the Mystery of the Bible is a resource of *The Great Adventure* Catholic Bible Study Program. It is the replacement study of *A Quick Journey Through the Bible.*

Jeff Cavins, General Editor, *The Great Adventure* Catholic Bible Study Program

Sarah Christmyer, Editor, *The Great Adventure* Catholic Bible Study Program, and Author, *Unlocking the Mystery of the Bible*

Ascension Press
Post Office Box 1990
West Chester, PA 19380
1-800-376-0520
AscensionPress.com
BibleStudyForCatholics.com

Cover design: Devin Schadt

Printed in the United States of America

ISBN 978-1-935940-88-3

Unlocking the Mystery of the Bible

Welcome to *The Great Adventure*

*"To fall in love with God is the greatest of all romances;
to seek him, the greatest adventure."*

– St. Augustine

The Bible is at the heart of our faith and our relationship with God. Much more than just another book, it is a "place" where our heavenly Father comes down to meet us and speaks to us with love.[1] Millions of people have found it to be a rich source of wisdom, encouragement, instruction, and solace.

Reading the Bible should bring us closer to Christ, but many people find it hard to even begin. *The Great Adventure* Catholic Bible Study Program and *The Bible Timeline* Learning System aim to make the complex simple—to give people a way to read the Bible and understand it … and so experience its life-changing power.

Since 2002, I have worked with Jeff Cavins in bringing *The Bible Timeline* Learning System to Catholics through various Bible studies and seminars. We are excited to offer this new *Great Adventure* study, *Unlocking the Mystery of the Bible.* Like its predecessor, *A Quick Journey Through the Bible,* this study seeks to draw you into God's marvelous plan of salvation as it unfolds throughout Sacred Scripture. It is my prayer that Jeff's dynamic teaching, in conjunction with the thought-provoking discussion questions and home Bible reading, will open the door to a newfound understanding of God's Word and his plan for your life.

Sarah Christmyer, Co-developer & Author, *The Great Adventure*

About *The Great Adventure* and *Unlocking the Mystery of the Bible*

At the core of *The Great Adventure* Catholic Bible Study Program is *The Bible Timeline* Learning System. *The Bible Timeline* presents a simple way of focusing on the story that runs throughout Scripture so that we can see the "big picture" of the Bible. This story is God's plan as it has unfolded in history and continues to unfold today. When we grasp this story, the Mass readings begin to make more sense, our Scripture reading and study come to life, and we see how our lives fit into God's loving plan.

Unlocking the Mystery of the Bible is the starting point of *The Great Adventure* Catholic Bible Study Program. In eight compelling videos, Jeff Cavins presents the story of salvation history from Creation and the Fall through the coming of Christ and the establishment of the Church. In this study, you will learn the story with the aid of an easy-to-use, color-coded *Bible Timeline* Chart and small-group discussion questions, which reinforce the video presentations and help you apply the message to your life.

Building on the basic understanding gained from this study is a series of Bible studies that explore the biblical narrative in light of Catholic teaching. Studies of individual books are supplemented by a growing number of studies on various themes and studies tailored for life application.

Unlocking the Mystery of the Bible replaces *A Quick Journey Through the Bible*. Because the content has been revised substantially, the workbooks and videos for *A Quick Journey Through the Bible* study are not compatible with *Unlocking the Mystery of the Bible*.

---

[1]   See Second Vatican Council, *Dei Verbum* (DV) 21.

Session Outline

Session (Video Times)	Title	Narrative Book(s)*
Session One (30:21)	Introduction	
(3:24)	*The Bible Timeline* Chart	
Session Two (33:01)	Early World	Genesis 1–11
Session Three (36:42)	Patriarchs	Genesis 12–50
Session Four (34:06)	Egypt and Exodus, Desert Wanderings	Exodus; Numbers
Session Five (31:03)	Conquest and Judges Royal Kingdom	Joshua; Judges 1 and 2 Samuel; 1 Kings 1–11
Session Six (30:49)	Divided Kingdom Exile Return	1 Kings 12–22; 2 Kings 2 Kings 17, 25 Ezra; Nehemiah
Session Seven (33:51)	Maccabean Revolt Messianic Fulfillment – Part 1	1 Maccabees Luke 1–21
Session Eight (34:20)	Messianic Fulfillment – Part 2 The Church Continuing the Journey	Luke 22–24 Acts

*"In *The Bible Timeline,* the term "narrative books" refers to fourteen books of the Bible that tell the story of salvation history from Creation through the establishment of the Church.

Materials

Unlocking the Mystery of the Bible includes the following materials:

- Eight, 30-minute **video presentations,** in which Jeff Cavins provides an overview and explanation of the twelve time periods of biblical history.

- **Student Workbook** *(one copy per participant),* which includes an introduction, Talk Notes, helpful maps and charts, small-group discussion questions, and home preparation for each session.

- **Leader's Guide** *(one copy for each leader and small-group facilitator),* which explains the approach of the study and provides instructions for leaders and facilitators. It also contains the full text of the *Unlocking the Mystery of the Bible* Student Workbook and includes suggested responses for the discussion questions.

The following materials are included with every Student Workbook and Leader's Guide:

- ***The Bible Timeline* Chart.** A color-coded, easy-to-use chart of salvation history that places key people and events in chronological order and divides them into twelve historical periods. It highlights the major biblical covenants, traces Christ's genealogy from Adam, and shows major events in world history. It can be folded to fit into a standard-size Bible.

- **The Bible Timeline Bookmark.** A quick-reference guide to the time periods to help you identify the books of the Bible that tell each stage of the "story." The Bookmark also illustrates the placement of the remaining fifty-nine books of the Bible and describes the meaning of the time period colors.

In addition, every participant should have a Catholic edition of the Bible. For recommendations on which version to use, see "Frequently Asked Questions" below.

Frequently Asked Questions

1. Which Bible should I use?

For this study, you will want to use a Catholic edition of the Bible, such as:

- Revised Standard Version–Catholic Edition (RSV-CE): a literal translation recommended for serious Bible study. This version is cited in the *Catechism of the Catholic Church* and is referenced in all *Bible Timeline* materials.

- New American Bible (NAB): a less literal, more "dynamic" translation that strives for readability; used in the *Lectionary* at Mass.

- New Jerusalem Bible (NJB): a "dynamic equivalent" translation that is less literal yet strives to be faithful to the original meaning.

2. How do I find a Scripture reference in my Bible?

Each book of the Bible is divided into chapters, and each chapter is made up of a series of numbered verses. To aid readers in finding a particular biblical verse, each Scripture passage has an "address," a location reference made up of the name of the Bible book, followed by the chapter and verse numbers. For example:

- 1 Samuel 7 refers to the entire seventh chapter of the book of 1 Samuel (pronounced "first Samuel" because there also is a 2 Samuel, or "second Samuel").

- Genesis 1:1 refers to the book of Genesis, Chapter 1, verse 1.

- Numbers 5:2-6 refers to the book of Numbers, Chapter 5, verses 2 through 6.

- I Corinthians 3:2-6, 7-10 refers to the book of 1 Corinthians ("first Corinthians"), Chapter 3, verses 2 through 6 and verses 7 through 10.

Abbreviations are often used in Scripture references. For example, "Jn 3:16" means "John, Chapter 3, verse 16." A list of abbreviations is found in the front of your Bible. To locate a particular book, use your Bible's contents page. As a general rule, *Great Adventure* Bible studies do not use Bible book abbreviations.

3. What is the Bible?

The Bible is the written expression of the Word of God. Although it contains seventy-three books written over many centuries by many different human authors in several languages, it is also a unified whole because all its books are inspired by the Holy Spirit, and together, they reveal God's plan of salvation.

Because God inspired the Bible's human authors, he is the principal Author of Scripture. As such, the Bible is inerrant ("without error"). As the Second Vatican Council's document on Sacred Scripture, *Dei Verbum* ("Word of God"), states:

Therefore, since everything asserted by the inspired authors or sacred writers must be held to be asserted by the Holy Spirit, it follows that the books of Scripture must be acknowledged as teaching solidly, faithfully and without error that truth which God wanted put into sacred writings for the sake of our salvation.[2]

4. What are the Old and New Testaments?

The books of the Bible are grouped under two headings—the Old Testament and the New Testament. The word "testament" can also be translated "covenant," which clarifies the meaning of these titles. The Old Testament tells how God made a series of "covenants" (i.e., binding agreements) with his people Israel in which he promised blessing in return for loving obedience. The New Testament tells how God fulfilled this promise of blessing by means of a new and everlasting covenant in his Son, Jesus Christ.

5. Why are Catholic and Protestant Bibles different?

Both Catholic and Protestant versions of the Bible contain the same twenty-seven books of the New Testament. It is the Old Testament that differs. The books of the New Testament are arranged in the following order:

- Four Gospels (Matthew, Mark, Luke, John) and the Acts of the Apostles

- St. Paul's letters (or "epistles") to the early Christian churches – Romans; 1 and 2 Corinthians; Galatians; Ephesians; Philippians; Colossians; 1 and 2 Thessalonians

- "Pastoral letters" – 1 and 2 Timothy; Titus; Philemon; Hebrews

- "Catholic letters" (James; 1 and 2 Peter; 1, 2, and 3 John; Jude) and the book of Revelation

In the early days of the Church, two versions of the Old Testament were used by the Jewish people. One, written entirely in Hebrew, contained thirty-nine books. The other, a Greek translation known as the Septuagint, contained forty-six books—the same thirty-nine as the Hebrew version plus another seven.

In AD 393, the bishops of the Church, with the authority given them by Christ, determined the list of inspired books of Scripture. This list contained the forty-six books of the Septuagint, which had been used by Christians since the first century. So, the Old Testament of the Church had forty-six books for more than a thousand years.

During the Protestant Reformation in the sixteenth century, the reformers chose to follow the shorter Hebrew collection of thirty-nine books. At the Council of Trent in 1546, the Septuagint's list of forty-six books was declared by the Catholic Church to be the "canon" (or "authoritative list of inspired books") of Scripture.

Here are the books of the Old Testament as found in Catholic versions of the Bible, listed by type of literature. The seven "deuterocanonical" books (which Protestants refer to as the "apocryphal books" or "the Apocrypha") are listed in italics:

---

2   DV 11. For more on canonicity, inspiration, and inerrancy, see the resources listed on page viii.

- Pentateuch – Genesis; Exodus; Leviticus; Numbers; Deuteronomy

- Historical books – Joshua; Judges; Ruth; 1 and 2 Samuel; 1 and 2 Kings; 1 and 2 Chronicles; Ezra; Nehemiah; *Tobit; Judith;* Esther; *1 and 2 Maccabees*

- Wisdom books – Job; Psalms; Proverbs; Ecclesiastes; Song of Solomon (Song of Songs), *Wisdom of Solomon; Sirach*

- Prophets – Isaiah; Jeremiah; Lamentations; *Baruch;* Ezekiel; Daniel; Hosea; Joel; Amos; Obadiah; Jonah; Micah; Nahum; Habakkuk; Zephaniah; Haggai; Zechariah; Malachi

Some deuterocanonical portions of Esther and Daniel are not included in Protestant versions.

6. What are the notes that appear in some Bibles?

The explanatory notes that appear in many versions of the Bible reflect the theological stance of their editors and the scholarship at the time of publication. All notes published in Catholic Bibles have received the *imprimatur* of a bishop, which is an official permission to publish that carries with it the assurance that nothing in the book is contrary to the faith or morality of the Church. (An *imprimatur* does not imply that the bishop who granted it agrees with the notes' content or that they are official Church teaching, however.) The notes are not considered part of Sacred Scripture and, therefore, are not divinely inspired.

7. Where can I find answers to my other questions about the Bible?

We recommend the following books and resources:

- The *Catechism of the Catholic Church.* For information about Sacred Scripture, its relationship to Sacred Tradition, and its inspiration and interpretation, see paragraphs 50 through 141. (The *Catechism* is available online and in published editions.)

- *Catholic Bible Dictionary,* Scott Hahn, general editor

- *The Bible Compass: A Catholic's Guide to Navigating the Scriptures,* by Edward Sri

- *Praying Scripture for a Change: An Introduction to Lectio Divina,* by Tim Gray

- *Walking with God: A Journey Through the Bible,* by Tim Gray and Jeff Cavins

Ten Commandments
of Small-Group Discussion

1. Enjoy yourself!

2. Speak with respect and charity.

3. Do not ridicule or dismiss what others say. Keep comments positive.

4. Come prepared.

5. If you were not able to prepare, let others speak first.

6. Stick to the topic and questions at hand.

7. Start and end on time.

8. Allow silence. Give people a chance to think.

9. Listen to others without interrupting.

10. Keep personal matters within the group.

Staying Focused

As you progress through *Unlocking the Mystery of the Bible,* you will probably come across things you want to know more about. It is exciting to learn how to read the Bible and explore its riches, but if you try to understand it all at once, you will become frustrated. The Bible is too big to understand all at once.

Unlocking the Mystery of the Bible makes the complex simple by initially setting aside many of the details to focus on the overall story—the "big picture"—of the Bible. Once you have this "big picture," you will have a framework to help you understand the entire Bible in its proper context.

The Bible is not a subject to master; it is a place to meet the living Word of God! Approach it with the goal of meeting God, and prepare to be transformed.

x

Session One

INTRODUCTION

Unlocking the Mystery of the Bible

Still Life with Bible, by Vincent van Gogh

Talk Notes

I. Welcome

A. About *Unlocking the Mystery of the Bible*

B. Catholics and the Bible

1. "In the sacred books, the Father who is in heaven meets his children with great love and speaks with them."[1]

2. Two keys: knowing God's heart and knowing his ways

3. The Church "exhorts" us to read the Bible (CCC 133)

II. The Problem …

A. The problem of the "heap": Catholicism can seem "big"

1. Four "pillars," or parts, of the *Catechism* help to organize the "heap"

a. The Creed

b. Sacraments and Liturgy

c. Life in Christ

d. Prayer

---

[1] DV 21.

2. The Creed (story) comes first

B. Not a book but a library

C. Other difficulties

III. ... And the Plan

A. Our need for a story

B. The key to reading the Bible: discovering the story

C. Making the complex simple

1. Sorting the "pile": twelve periods

2. Keeping it simple: fourteen narrative books

3. Making it memorable: *The Bible Timeline* Chart

4. Tools for the journey

- Takeaways -

1. **The Bible tells a love story of God reaching out to you.**

2. **Get a Bible. Get away. Get together with God.**

Discussion Questions

1. The Church tells us: "In the sacred books, the Father who is in heaven meets his children with great love and speaks with them."[2] Have you experienced this? In the video presentation, Jeff mentioned common difficulties people have when they start to read the Bible. What has been your experience with Scripture?

2. Many Catholics today feel as though they have received a "heap of Catholicism," a random pile of separate Bible stories and facts about the Church's teachings. What solution to this problem do the four "pillars" of the *Catechism* offer?

3. Why is it important to get the "big picture" of salvation history before reading or studying the Bible?

---

[2] DV 21.

Overview of Salvation History

The stories in the Old and New Testaments are not disconnected, random events in the history of a people. Rather, each story presents a crucial part of God's plan. By the end of this study, you will see the "narrative thread" that runs throughout Scripture and continues in your life today.

The Bible Timeline Chart groups the stories into twelve consecutive historical periods that are color coded to help you remember them. Look at each period on *The Bible Timeline* Chart while someone reads the story in outline form as follows:

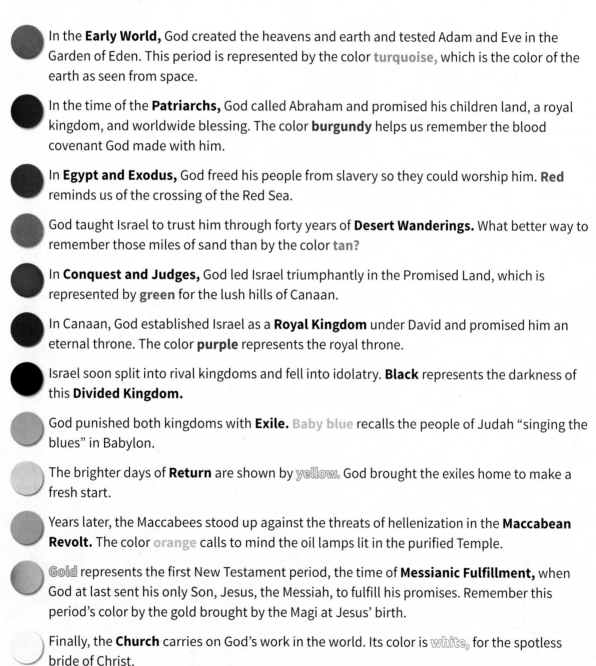

In the **Early World,** God created the heavens and earth and tested Adam and Eve in the Garden of Eden. This period is represented by the color turquoise, which is the color of the earth as seen from space.

In the time of the **Patriarchs,** God called Abraham and promised his children land, a royal kingdom, and worldwide blessing. The color **burgundy** helps us remember the blood covenant God made with him.

In **Egypt and Exodus,** God freed his people from slavery so they could worship him. **Red** reminds us of the crossing of the Red Sea.

God taught Israel to trust him through forty years of **Desert Wanderings.** What better way to remember those miles of sand than by the color **tan?**

In **Conquest and Judges,** God led Israel triumphantly in the Promised Land, which is represented by **green** for the lush hills of Canaan.

In Canaan, God established Israel as a **Royal Kingdom** under David and promised him an eternal throne. The color **purple** represents the royal throne.

Israel soon split into rival kingdoms and fell into idolatry. **Black** represents the darkness of this **Divided Kingdom.**

God punished both kingdoms with **Exile.** Baby blue recalls the people of Judah "singing the blues" in Babylon.

The brighter days of **Return** are shown by yellow. God brought the exiles home to make a fresh start.

Years later, the Maccabees stood up against the threats of hellenization in the **Maccabean Revolt.** The color orange calls to mind the oil lamps lit in the purified Temple.

Gold represents the first New Testament period, the time of **Messianic Fulfillment,** when God at last sent his only Son, Jesus, the Messiah, to fulfill his promises. Remember this period's color by the gold brought by the Magi at Jesus' birth.

Finally, the **Church** carries on God's work in the world. Its color is white, for the spotless bride of Christ.

4.   The "narrative books" section of *The Bible Timeline* Chart gives you the names of fourteen books of the Bible that tell the story of salvation history from beginning to end. They are arranged across the top of the Chart immediately below the period names, so you can see the historical time periods they describe. List the narrative books here.

5.   Fifty-nine "supplemental books" make up the rest of the Bible. These books are not designated "supplemental" because they are less important than the narrative books; but in this study, we will set them aside to focus on the "big picture." Once you have learned the chronological story told in these narrative books, you will be better equipped to read the remaining books of the Bible in their historical context.

Look at the top of the purple Royal Kingdom period on your Chart. The books of 1 Samuel 9–31, 2 Samuel, and 1 Kings 1–11 tell the story of this time period, during which God established a kingdom under David and Solomon. What are the "supplemental books" for this time period? (You can find these listed at the bottom of the Royal Kingdom period on your *Bible Timeline* Chart.)

6.   God's formation of his family through covenants with various people is central to the story of the Bible. These covenants are marked by white stars at the top of the Chart in a section called "God's Family Plan." You will learn more about these later, but notice the type of family group name with each star ("One Holy Couple," for example). What do you notice about the change in this family group as you move from left to right across the Chart?

7.   Key people and events in salvation history are arranged in chronological order along the center of the *Timeline* Chart. This section is divided into three horizontal bands representing different aspects of the Middle East. The central area represents the land of Canaan, where most of the events in the story take place. When the action moves out of Canaan—to the northern countries like Babylon, for example, or to the south and Egypt—the events appear above or below the center area. Look at your Chart: What examples of geographic movement do you see?

8.   Check out the events in secular history that are arranged across the bottom of the Chart. Find one you are familiar with. What is going on in the development of God's plan during this period?

Closing Prayer

*God's plan unfolded through history and gives us the "story"
for our lives. Let us pray in the name of Jesus:*

R: *Speak to us as we read your Word!*

Home Preparation: Looking Ahead

Every story has a beginning, middle, and end. The story of salvation history begins at the dawn of time. In the Early World period, you will learn how the world began, what went terribly wrong, and how God promised to provide a solution.

- Use your Chart to fill in the following information:

    Period name: _____**Early World**_____ Approximate dates: _____

    Period color: _____ Color meaning: _____

    List four key people from Jesus' genealogy:

    1) _____   3) _____

    2) _____   4) _____

    List five key events:

    1) _____   4) _____

    2) _____   5) _____

    3) _____

    Name one concurrent event in secular history: _____

- The story of the Early World is found in Genesis 1–11. You probably know these stories already, although you may not know how they are connected. We will explain that in the next session. In the meantime, read one or more of them ahead of time, in preparation.

    ### Early World:

    Genesis 1–3 . . . . Creation, Adam and Eve, the Fall
    Genesis 4 . . . . Cain and Abel
    Genesis 6, 9 . . . . Noah and the Flood
    Genesis 11:1-9 . . . . The Tower of Babel

Understanding *The Bible Timeline* Chart

- Take a few moments to familiarize yourself with the parts of the Chart by reading the "Key to Understanding the *The Bible Timeline* Chart" on the inside front cover of your Chart, and following along with *The Bible Timeline* Chart video in *Unlocking the Mystery of the Bible* video series.

- Review the twelve historic periods by filling in their names and the meanings of their associated colors in the chart below.

Period Name	Color	Color Meaning
1.		
2.		
3.		
4.		
5.		
6.		
7.		
8.		
9.		
10.		
11.		
12.		

- Find the Contents page in your Bible. Using your *Bible Timeline* Chart or Bookmark as a reference, highlight the fourteen narrative books. If you are not accustomed to finding books in your Bible, take time to locate each narrative book before you continue.

Session Two

EARLY WORLD

Genesis 1-11

Setting the Plot for the Rest of the Story

Talk Notes

I. Introduction

    A. The Early World on the Chart

    B. Reading Genesis 1–11, "a certain type of history"

II. Creation (Genesis 1–2)

    A. The earth

        1. Days 1-3: God brings form

        2. Days 4-6: God fills the void

    B. Humanity

        1. Image and likeness (reason, will, capacity for love)

        2. Male and female

        3. Stipulations

III. The Fall (Genesis 3)

    A. The lie of the Enemy: You can be like God without God

    B. The first sin: lack of trust in God (CCC 397)

        1. St. Thomas Aquinas: Pride is disordered self-trust

    C. The "DNA" of sin (Genesis 3:6-7)

        1. Good for food, a delight to the eyes, makes one wise

        2. Focus on the creation versus the Creator

        3. St. Augustine's example of stolen pears

    D. Original sin: intellect darkened, will weakened, concupiscence

    E. God has a plan: Genesis 3:15 (*Protoevangelium*, "first gospel")

    F. Do you trust God?

1. St. John Paul II: "practical atheism"[1]

G. Exile "East of Eden," guard on the Tree of Life

1. John 6: The Cross becomes the Tree of Life, its fruit the Eucharist

2. **KEY:** the pattern of exile

H. The results of sin

1. Changed relationship with God

2. Changed relationship with each other

3. Changed relationship with the earth

IV. After the Fall (Genesis 6–11)

A. The Flood (Chapters 6–9)

1. God "repents"

2. A new beginning: covenant with Noah

B. The world is populated (Chapter 10)

C. The Tower of Babel (Chapter 11)

V. Conclusion

A. There is hope: God has a plan

B. Genealogies focus the story

- Takeaways -

1. God does not give up on broken lives.

2. God has a plan, and it includes you.

---

[1] St. John Paul II, General Audience, April 14, 1999.

Discussion Questions

1. The story of the Early World is told in **Genesis 1–11.** Locate the Early World period on your *Bible Timeline* Chart. Who are the main characters, and what are the main events?

2. What does mankind's first sin consist of?

3. What are the consequences of the Fall for Adam and Eve and for us?

4. How do you see those consequences in the lives of the people that follow?

5. Turn to **Genesis 3:15** in your Bible. What hope that the situation will be redeemed is given at the outset of the story?

6. In the story of Noah, we see God deal with the mounting wickedness by destroying the earth with a flood. Does that "solution" to the problem work? Why, or why not?

7. Describe the condition of mankind at the close of the Early World period, following the Tower of Babel incident.

8. Do you trust God, or are you tempted, like Adam and Eve, to put your trust in yourself or in created things? What did you learn from Jeff's talk that challenges or helps you?

Closing Prayer

God's plan unfolded through history and gives us the "story"
for our lives. Let us pray in the name of Jesus.

In the Early World, you created the heavens and earth
and tested Adam and Eve in the Garden:

***R:** Help us to always choose the life you offer.*

Our Father …

Home Preparation: Looking Ahead

By the end of the Early World period, Adam and Eve's descendants have spread throughout the known world. For the rest of the book of Genesis (which narrates the period of the Patriarchs) the story focuses on the family of one man, Abraham, with whom God will establish an everlasting promise of blessing. His descendants will be God's Chosen People, Israel, and through them, God will bless the entire world.

- Use your Chart to fill in the following information about this time period:

    Period name: _____*Patriarchs*_____ Approximate dates: _____

    Period color: _____ Color meaning: _____

    List four key people from the Patriarch's period:

    1) _____

    2) _____

    3) _____

    4) _____

    What is the most important event? _____

    What nation is the current world power? _____

- The story of the Patriarchs period is full of action and many memorable stories, some of them central not just to Israel's history but to the history of the Church as well. If you do not have time to read Genesis 12–50, try reading one or more of the following passages.

    ### Patriarchs:

    Genesis 12:1-9 . . . . God calls Abraham

    Genesis 15, 17, 22 . . . . . God's covenant with Abraham

    Genesis 25:19-34 . . . . . . Jacob and Esau

    Genesis 29:1–30:24 . . . . Jacob gets married; Jacob's children

    Genesis 32:22-32 . . . . . . Jacob wrestles with God and gets a new name

    Genesis 37–50. . . . . Joseph and his brothers: to just get the gist of the story, focus on Chapters 37 and 41–44

Session Three

PATRIARCHS

Genesis 12-50

God's Everlasting Promise to Abraham

Sacrifice of Isaac, by Caravaggio

Talk Notes

I.   **Introduction: Patriarchs on the Chart**

II. **God Calls Abram Out of Ur (Genesis 12)**

    A. Significance of the land

    B. God's promise to Abraham

        1. Three promises (Genesis 12:1-3)

        2. Problem: childlessness (Genesis 15)

        3. Abraham's faith

            a. Abraham: our father in the Faith (Galatians 3:7)

    C. The meaning of covenant

III. **Isaac and Ishmael (Genesis 16–22)**

    A. Abraham prepares to sacrifice Isaac (Chapter 22)

    B. **KEY:** Looking for God's Lamb

IV. **Jacob and Esau (Genesis 27–36)**

    A. Birthright and blessing

        1. Esau sells his birthright

            a. Esau is a "profane" man (see Hebrews 12:16, NAB)

            b. What is your "lentil soup"?

        2. Jacob steals the blessing

    B. Exile and marriage

    C. Wrestling and name change: "Jacob" to "Israel"

        1. **KEY:** Twelve sons become twelve tribes

V. Joseph and Judah (Genesis 37–50)

    A. Joseph is sold into slavery

    B. Joseph in prison

    C. Joseph is raised to power

        1. *al ha-bayit,* "over the household"

        2. New Testament connection: Peter

    D. Judah's story (Genesis 37): contrast with Joseph

    E. Two visits to Egypt

        1. Judah's transformation

        2. What they mean for evil, God means for good

VI. Jacob Blesses His Sons (Genesis 49)

- Takeaways -

1. You can believe and trust God.

2. God uses difficult circumstances to do marvelous things.

THE COVENANTAL STRUCTURE OF SALVATION HISTORY

The charts below diagram the way salvation history unfolded through a series of covenants God made with his people. Adam and Eve were created in a close relationship with God that was shattered at the Fall. This relationship with God would later be imaged by families and bonds of kinship created through covenantal promises. God moved to restore humanity to relationship with himself by means of a series of covenants.

The first diagram shows how God expands on aspects of the initial promise he made to Abraham in Genesis 12. Each of these covenantal promises to Abraham and his descendants (of land, kingdom, and worldwide blessing) would be fulfilled in a future covenant: the Mosaic Covenant, the Davidic Covenant, and the New Covenant in Jesus Christ.

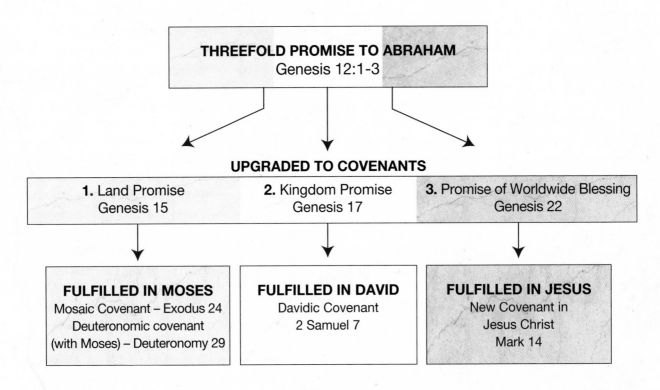

The following diagram shows the progressive growth of God's family from "One Holy Couple" to "One, Holy, Catholic, and Apostolic Church," illustrated by means of these same covenants.

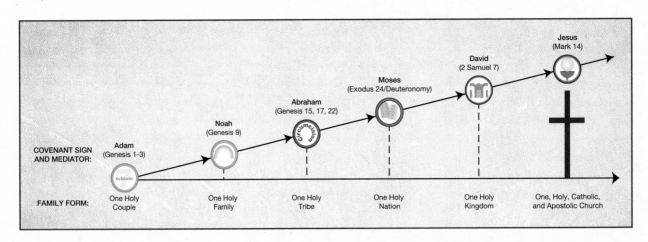

ABRAHAM'S JOURNEY

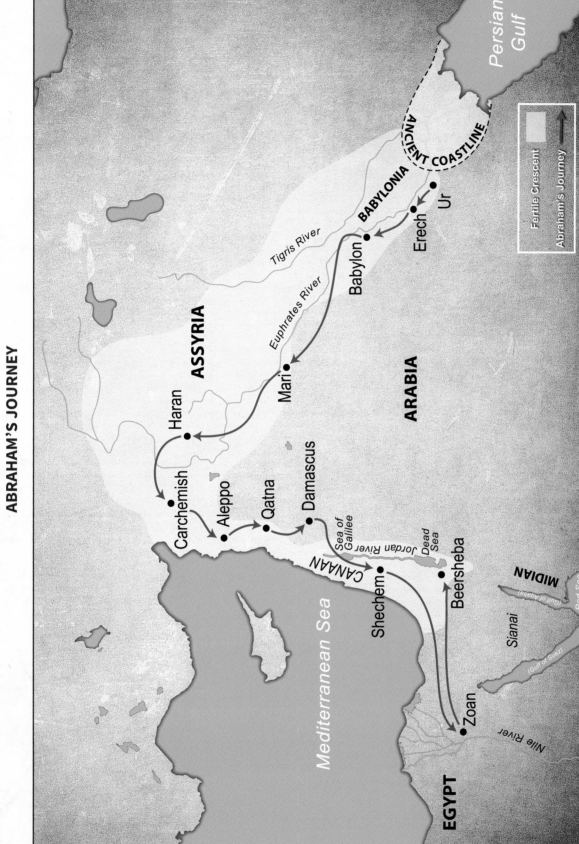

DISCUSSION QUESTIONS

1. Mankind has been scattered and their languages confused after they tried to build a name for themselves rather than calling on the name of the LORD. What is God's first step toward restoring them to himself? (See **Genesis 12:1-3.**)

2. "Patriarchs" means literally, "fathers" in the same sense we use the terms "forefathers" or "Founding Fathers." This period tells of the patriarchs—the "founding fathers"—of the nation of Israel. Who are they?

3. Why is the color burgundy used to represent this time period?

4. Read **Genesis 12:1-3.** What promises does God make to Abraham?

5. To whom do the promises pass in the following generations?

6. God's three covenant promises to Abraham are elaborated in **Genesis 15, 17, and 22.** In this three-part covenant (also called the "Abrahamic Covenant"), God promises to give Abraham's descendants a land, to establish them as a kingdom, and to make them a source of worldwide blessing. This covenant gives us a blueprint for understanding the rest of the Bible, which is basically the story of God making good on those promises. Look at the Patriarchs period on your Chart to get an idea of where the story is headed. Each time God fulfills one of the promises, he makes yet another covenant with his people. Find the "Abrahamic Covenant" box on your Chart, and identify the people through whom God will make future covenants with his people and fulfill the three promises he made to Abraham.

Land Promise:

Kingdom Promise:

Promise of Worldwide Blessing:

7. Throughout salvation history, God repeatedly poses the same question to mankind: "Will you trust me?" What does trust in God look like, as demonstrated in the life of Abraham?

8. How might God be calling you to trust in him today?

Closing Prayer

*God's plan unfolded through history and gives us the "story"
for our lives. Let us pray in the name of Jesus.*

*In the time of the Patriarchs, you called Abraham and promised
his children land, a royal kingdom, and worldwide blessing:*

R: *Help us to always hope in your promises.*

Our Father …

Home Preparation: Looking Ahead

The next session will cover two time periods. On your Bible Timeline *Chart, you will note that the first time period covered, Egypt and Exodus, spans approximately four hundred years. Little is known about much of this time. When our story opens, Jacob's family (also called "Israel") has been in Egypt for generations. When a new pharaoh comes to power and enslaves them, they cry out to God for deliverance. God takes them out of Egypt and in the process, punishes the Egyptians and demonstrates his power through the dramatic events of the Passover. He then establishes Israel as his own people, "a kingdom of priests and a holy nation."*

Despite the many miracles God works to free Israel from slavery, his people refuse to trust him. The following forty-year period of Desert Wanderings is both a punishment and an opportunity for them to learn to trust God in preparation for conquering and living in the land of Canaan.

- Use your Chart to fill in the following information about these time periods:

    Period name: _____*Egypt and Exodus*_____ Approximate dates: _____

    Period color: _____ Color meaning: _____

    Supplemental book for this period: _____

    What key person does God send?: _____

    Name a current event in secular history: _____

    Period name: _____*Desert Wanderings*_____ Approximate dates: _____

    Period color: _____ Color meaning: _____

    List two key events: _____ _____

    Narrative book for this period: _____

- In the future, you may want to read all of the books of Exodus and Numbers. For now, choose one or more of the following passages to read before the next meeting to give you a feel for these time periods.

    Egypt and Exodus:

    Exodus 3 . . . . Moses and the burning bush

    Exodus 7–10 . . . . Plagues on Egypt

    Exodus 11–14 . . . . The last plague (Passover), the Exodus, the Red Sea

    Exodus 32 . . . . The golden calf

    Desert Wanderings:

    Numbers 13–14 . . . . Rebellion and forty years of wandering

    Numbers 25 . . . . Israel's apostasy with the Baal of Peor

Session Four

EGYPT AND EXODUS

Exodus

God Leads Israel Out of Bondage

DESERT WANDERINGS

Numbers

Israel Must Learn to Trust God

Crossing of the Red Sea, by Jacques Courtois

Talk Notes

I.   **Egypt and Exodus and Desert Wanderings on the Chart**

II.   **Egypt and Exodus**

A. Release from Egypt (Exodus 1–15)

1. Israel cries out to God (Chapter 1)

2. God raises up Moses (Chapter 2)

a. "Moses" is from the Hebrew *moshe,* "to draw out" (of water)

b. Moses flees to the desert

3. Burning bush (Chapter 3)

a. "I AM" – "I AM WHO I AM" (tetragrammaton, YHWH, or "Yahweh")

b. God sends Moses to Pharaoh

4. Plagues on Egypt (Chapters 7–10)

5. The Passover

a. The central redemptive event in Israel's history

i. Freedom

ii. Provision

iii. God's presence

iv. Liturgy and worship, intimacy with God

v. "Boot camp"

b. The lamb

6. The Exodus

a. Crossing the Red Sea

b. Heading south to Sinai (three months)

        i.   God demonstrates faithfulness

        ii.   God provides *manna* ("what is it?")

  B. Covenant at Sinai

    1. "One Holy Nation" (Exodus 19:6; 1 Peter 2:9)

    2. The broken covenant: Someone has to die

    3. One year of formation

      a. Tabernacle: a pattern of worship

      b. Law (in context of covenant)

      c. Levitical priesthood (after the golden calf incident)

III. Desert Wanderings

  A. Kadesh-barnea: twelve spies sent out (Numbers 13)

    1. Failure to trust God

    2. Forty years in the desert, learning to trust (Numbers 14–36)

  B. Moses strikes the rock

  C. Moses' last words: Deuteronomy

    1. *Shema Israel* – "The Lord our God is one Lord" (Deuteronomy 6:4)

    2. Teach your children

IV. Conclusion: God Has Been Raising His "Firstborn Son," a "Holy Nation"

- Takeaways -

1. We need to teach our children.

2. Scripture was written for our instruction to give us hope (see Romans 15:4).

3. God hears your cry.

PROPOSED ROUTE OF THE EXODUS AND DESERT WANDERINGS
(The precise route is not known.)

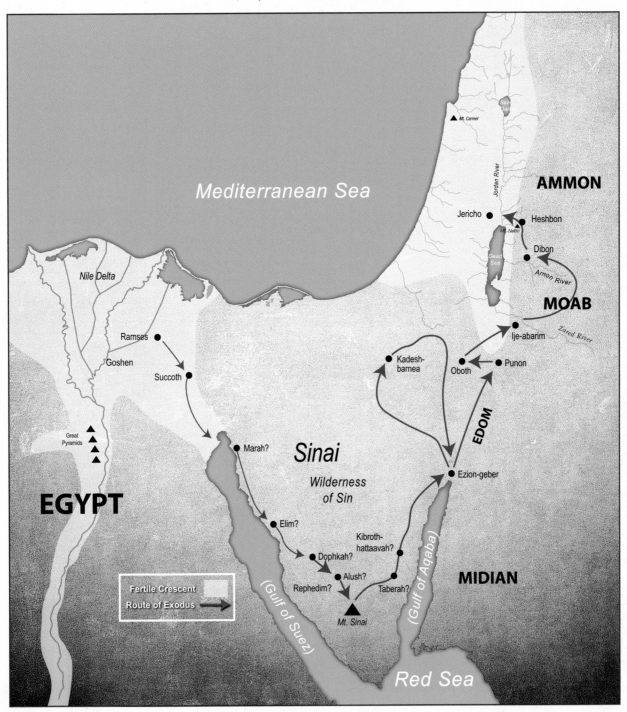

PLAN OF THE TABERNACLE (EXODUS 40:16-34) AND ARRANGEMENT OF TRIBAL CAMPS (NUMBERS 2)

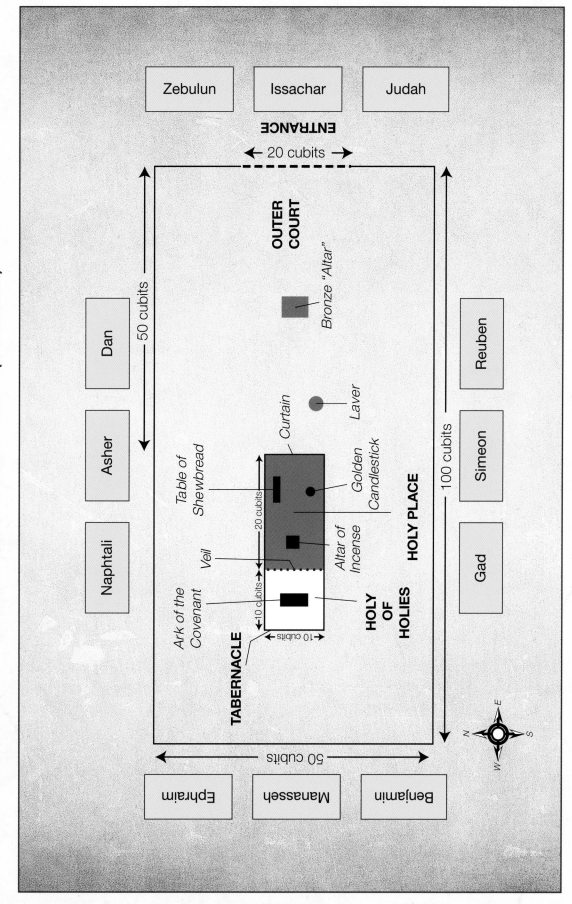

Discussion Questions

1. In the episode of the burning bush, God introduces himself to Moses as "the God of Abraham, the God of Isaac, and the God of Jacob" (see **Exodus 3:6**). What does that tell Moses about God?

2. What important message do the ten plagues send to Egypt and Israel?

3. God tells Pharaoh that if he does not free Israel, God's firstborn son, then he will kill the firstborn sons of Egypt. How does the Lord accomplish this? What is the name of the annual remembrance of this event?

4. **Think About It:** In the Red Sea crossing, the children of Israel are freed from their enemy by passing through water. What sacrament of the New Covenant does this event prefigure? Explain.

5. The first terms of the Sinai Covenant are what we know as the Ten Commandments. St. John Paul II called the Ten Commandments "the law of freedom: not the freedom to follow our blind passions, but the freedom to love, to choose what is good in every situation, even when to do so is a burden."[1] Think about the Ten Commandments (see **Exodus 20**). What kinds of "false gods" do they free us from?

[1] Pope John Paul II, "Celebration of the Word at Mount Sinai," St. Catherine's Monastery, February 26, 2000.

6. Jeff describes the year at Mount Sinai as a "hinge point" for Israel, during which God gives the people three things. What are those three things?

7. What does the Tabernacle signify to Israel?

8. Why does God make Israel wander for forty years in the desert? What is he trying to teach the people?

9. St. Paul tells us that these stories have been "written down for our instruction" (see **1 Corinthians 10:11**). What message do these stories hold for you today?

Closing Prayer

God's plan unfolded through history and gives us the "story"
for our lives. Let us pray in the name of Jesus.

You freed your people from slavery in Egypt so they could worship you:

R: Free us from sin so we can serve and worship you.

You taught Israel to walk in faith through forty
years wandering in the desert:

R: Help us to trust in you, O God.

Our Father …

Home Preparation: Looking Ahead

The next session will cover two periods, Conquest and Judges and Royal Kingdom. After forty years in the desert, Israel enters Canaan, the Promised Land. God's first promise to Abraham is fulfilled. However, Israel's failure to keep God's commandments leads to sin, oppression, and an incomplete possession of the land.

*The people of Israel grow weary of being led by judges and demand a king "like all the nations" (see **1 Samuel 8:5**). God's second promise to Abraham—that of an everlasting royal kingdom—is fulfilled in King David.*

- Use your Chart to fill in the following information about these time periods:

  Period name: _____*Conquest and Judges*_____ Approximate dates: _____

  Period color: _____ Color meaning: _____

  Narrative books: _____

  List any names familiar to you and tell what you know about them:

  _____

  _____

  Period name: _____*Royal Kingdom*_____ Approximate dates: _____

  Period color: _____ Color meaning: _____

  Key people: _____

  What would you say is the key event? _____

- It is difficult to narrow down the reading because so many wonderful stories take place during the periods of Conquest and Judges and Royal Kingdom. Read some or all of the following passages to get an overview of these two time periods. Make sure to return to this important stage in God's plan sometime in the future.

  ### Conquest and Judges:

  Joshua 2 . . . . Rahab and the spies

  Joshua 6 . . . . The Fall of Jericho

  Judges 1:1–3:6 . . . . Conquest; overview of sin cycle

  Judges 13–16 . . . . Samson and Delilah

  ### Royal Kingdom:

  1 Samuel 8 . . . . Israel asks for a king

  2 Samuel 7 . . . . God makes a covenant with David

  1 Kings 9, 11:1-13 . . . . . . Solomon's reign and folly

THE CONQUEST OF CANAAN

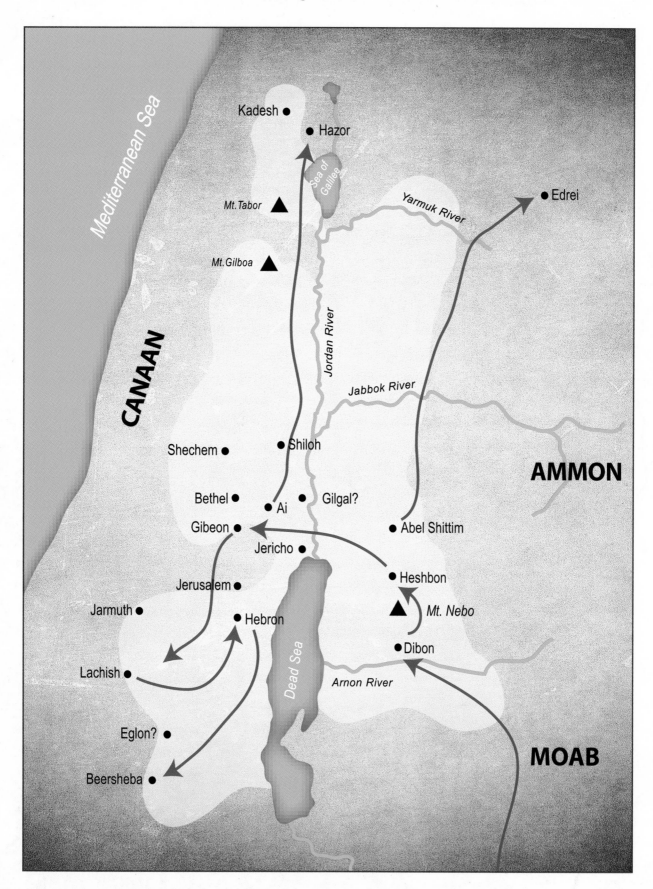

Mediterranean Sea

Kadesh ●

● Hazor

Sea of Galilee

Mt. Tabor ▲

Edrei ●

Yarmuk River

Mt. Gilboa ▲

Jordan River

Jabbok River

CANAAN

Shechem ●   ● Shiloh

AMMON

Bethel ●   ● Ai   Gilgal?

Gibeon ●

Jericho ●   ● Abel Shittim

Jerusalem ●   ● Heshbon

Jarmuth ●   ▲ *Mt. Nebo*

Hebron ●   ● Dibon

Dead Sea

Lachish ●   *Arnon River*

Eglon? ●

MOAB

Beersheba ●

ISRAEL – THE TWELVE TRIBES

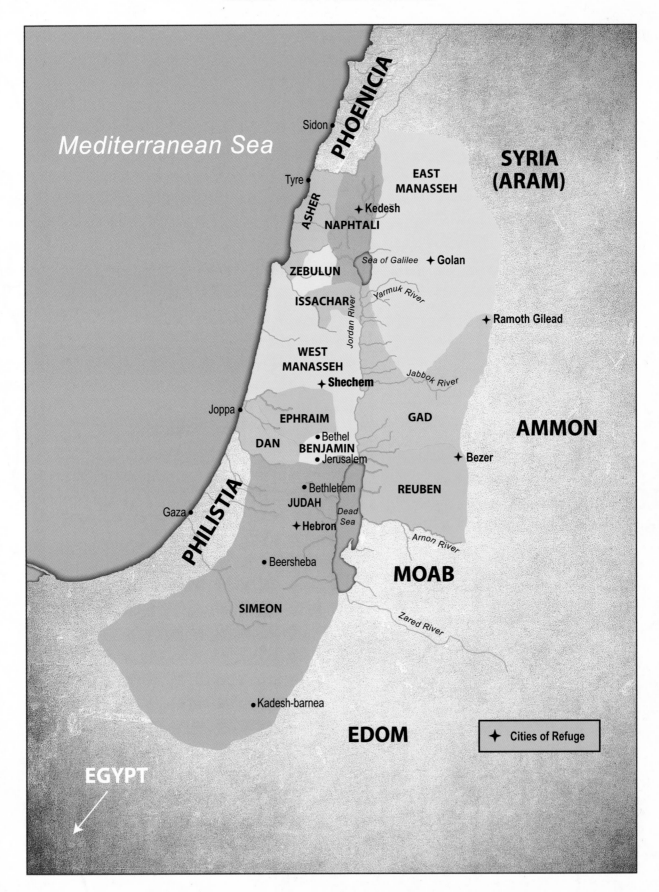

Session Five

CONQUEST AND JUDGES

Joshua, Judges

Israel Enters the Promised Land

ROYAL KINGDOM

1 and 2 Samuel, 1 Kings 1-2

God Establishes a Kingdom in Israel

Hill Country of Judea

Talk Notes

I.   **Review: The Story So Far**

II. **Conquest and Judges**

    A. Conquest and Judges on the Chart

    B. The Conquest of Canaan (Joshua)

        1. Israel crosses the Jordan (Chapter 3)

        2. The fall of Jericho (Chapter 6)

            a. *Herem* warfare

        3. Covenant renewal

        4. Conquest strategy: divide and conquer

        5. Incomplete conquest

        6. Tribal allotment

        7. "Every man did what was right in his own eyes" (Judges 21:25)

    C. Judges (book of Judges)

        1. Death of Joshua

        2. Sevenfold cycle: sin – servitude – supplication – salvation – silence

        3. Twelve judges

      a. Deborah

      b. Samson: microcosm of the macro reality

  4. Supplemental book for Judges: Ruth

  5. The last judge: Samuel

      a. Israel asks for a king (1 Samuel 8:4-5)

      b. Consequences

      c. What they need, wrapped in what they want

III. Royal Kingdom

  A. Royal Kingdom on the Chart

  B. Saul unites the kingdom

      1. Saul from the Hebrew *Sha'ul* ("asked for"), tribe of Benjamin

      2. Saul sins, loses the kingdom (see 1 Samuel 13:13-14)

  C. David expands the kingdom

      1. David is anointed

      2. David kills Goliath

      3. David sins, repents (Psalm 51)

4. God's Covenant with David (2 Samuel 7)

    a. I will make *your* name great (royal dynasty)

    b. **KEY:** Jesus will assume the throne of David

D. Solomon builds the kingdom

    1. Supplemental books: 1 and 2 Chronicles and the wisdom literature

    2. First Temple is built

    3. Solomon becomes a tyrant

        a. Deuteronomy 17:14-17

        b. 1 Kings 10–12

E. Ahijah's prophecy to Jeroboam (1 Kings 11:29-32)

    1. The kingdom will be torn in two

    2. A portion will remain for David's line

IV. Use *The Bible Timeline* Chart to Find Your Place in the Story

> # - Takeaways -
>
> **1. God can change the world through the most unlikely people.**
>
> **2. God wants to be enthroned on your heart.**

Discussion Questions

1. Before he dies, Moses tells Israel how to live in order to receive God's blessing in the Promised Land. Read **Deuteronomy 6:4-9** (see the green box on this page). Observant Jews today pray this passage, known as the *Shema,* every morning and evening. In Israel's conquest of the land, do they follow Moses' instructions? What happens?

> **The *Shema*
> (Deuteronomy 6:4-9)**
>
> "Hear, O Israel: The Lord our God is one Lord; and you shall love the Lord your God with all your heart, and with all your soul, and with all your might. And these words which I command you this day shall be upon your heart; and you shall teach them diligently to your children, and shall talk of them when you sit in your house, and when you walk by the way, and when you lie down, and when you rise. And you shall bind them as a sign upon your hand, and they shall be as frontlets between your eyes. And you shall write them on the doorposts of your house and on your gates."

2. How well does Israel follow God's command to possess the land of Canaan?

3. Explain the sevenfold cycle Israel experiences during the time of Conquest and Judges.

4. At the close of the period of Conquest and Judges, what plea does Israel make?

5. Who is the first king of Israel? How does he fare?

6. Read **2 Samuel 7:1-16.** How does the Davidic covenant fulfill and expand upon God's second promise to Abraham?

7. King Solomon is the wisest man who ever lived. What causes him to turn away from God? (see **1 Kings 11:4-6.**)

8. God says David is "a man after his own heart" (see **1 Samuel 13:14**). Based on this description, what qualities do you think David has?

A man after God's own heart "who," God said, "will do all my ~~will~~ will" (See Acts 13:22), which types and foreshadows Jesus who prayed in the Garden of Gethsemane, "Father, if though art willing, remove this cup from me, nevertheless not my will, but thine be done" (Luke 22:42).

Closing Prayer

*God's plan unfolded through history and gives us the "story"
for our lives. Let us pray in the name of Jesus.*

*You led Israel triumphantly into the Promised Land. They failed to teach
their children and instead did what was right in their own eyes:*

R: *Help us to keep our eyes on you and bring up our children in your way.*

*You established a kingdom on your servant David
and promised him an eternal throne:*

R: *Establish your kingdom in our midst.*

Our Father …

Home Preparation: Review

We are now halfway through The Bible Timeline *Chart. Take a moment to review the periods you have covered so far, using your Chart or Bookmark. What are the period names? What does each color stand for? Record a simple phrase you can use to remember what each period is about. (You may use titles from each session or make up your own.) Fill out the chart below. If you need help, see page 5 for ideas.*

	Period Name	Color	Color Meaning	Phrase
1.				
2.				
3.				
4.				
5.				
6.				

Home Preparation: Looking Ahead

King Solomon's son Rehoboam increases the oppressive policies of his father, and the people revolt. The kingdom divides into two separate kingdoms—Israel in the North, Judah in the South—and the kingdom of Israel is irrevocably changed.

The division of the kingdom leads to idolatry and wickedness. Israel and Judah's spiritual separation from God leads to physical separation from their land in a period of foreign exile. A remnant of God's people will return to the Promised Land after seventy years in exile. In the Return, they will work hard to rebuild what they lost through sin and idolatry.

- Use your Chart to fill in the following information about these three time periods:

  Period name: _____ **Divided Kingdom** _____ Approximate dates: _____

  Period color: _____ Color meaning: _____

  The two kingdoms are represented on the *Timeline* Chart by two horizontal bars: the Northern Kingdom of _____, its capital at _____ ; and the Southern Kingdom of _____, its capital at _____.

  Period name: _____ **Exile** _____ Approximate dates: _____

  Period color: _____ Color meaning: _____

  New world power: _____

  List three events found in the parchment-colored boxes during the Exile period on your Chart:

  1) _____

  2) _____

  3) _____

  Period name: _____ **Return** _____ Approximate dates: _____

  Period color: _____ Color meaning: _____

  Apart from the actual return to the land itself, what important events characterize this time? (Read events 49, 50, and 52.)

  _____

  _____

  Prophets during this time: _____

  Two new world powers: _____ _____

- The readings for the period of the Divided Kingdom are complex because of the number of people involved and because the story swings back and forth between events in Israel (in the North) and Judah (in the South). The following passages will focus your attention on the reason for the split and give you an understanding of why and how the people go into exile. Readings from the prophets (supplemental books for this period) are included. These prophets demonstrate God's love for his disobedient children.

Divided Kingdom:

1 Kings 11:26–13:10, 14 . . The Royal Kingdom divides; sins of the North

Hosea 11, 14 . . . . A message to the North (Israel; also called "Ephraim")

Jeremiah 31:1-14 . . . . A message to the South (Judah)

Exile:

2 Kings 17 . . . . Exile of the North (Israel)

2 Kings 25:1-21 . . . . Exile of the South (Judah)

Return:

Ezra 1, 3 . . . . Cyrus foretold; the Return; foundations of the Temple laid

Ezra 4–6 . . . . Samaritan opposition

Nehemiah 1, 2, 6 . . . . Nehemiah's return; rebuilding of Jerusalem walls

The Flight of the Prisoners, by James Jacques Joseph Tissot

THE DIVIDED KINGDOM
(930–586 BC)

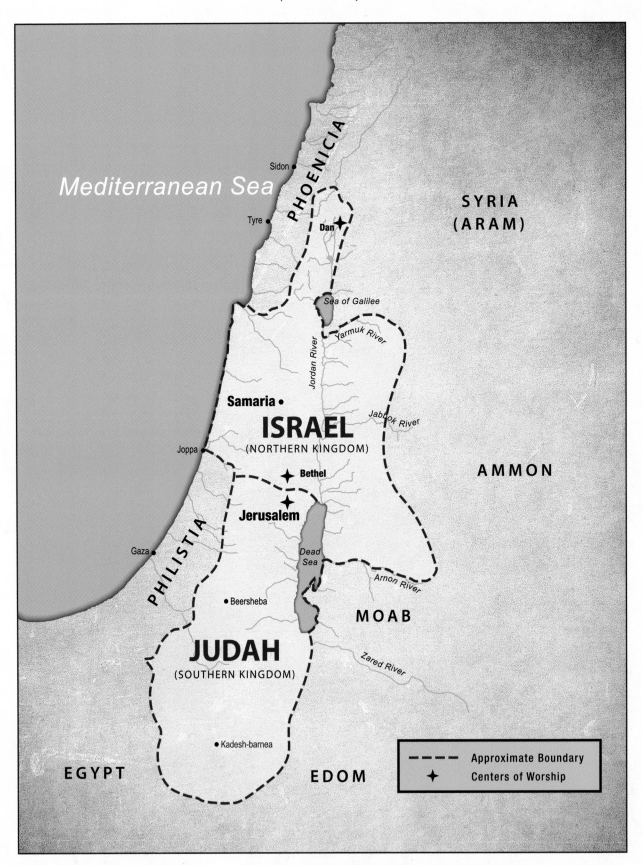

Mediterranean Sea

PHOENICIA

Sidon

Tyre

Dan

SYRIA (ARAM)

Sea of Galilee

Yarmuk River

Jordan River

Samaria

ISRAEL
(NORTHERN KINGDOM)

Jabbok River

Joppa

AMMON

Bethel

Jerusalem

Gaza

Dead Sea

PHILISTIA

Arnon River

Beersheba

MOAB

JUDAH
(SOUTHERN KINGDOM)

Zared River

Kadesh-barnea

EGYPT

EDOM

- - - Approximate Boundary
✦ Centers of Worship

DIVIDED KINGDOM

1 Kings 12-22, 2 Kings

Tyranny Leads to Division

EXILE

2 Kings

God's People Are Removed from the Promised Land

RETURN

Ezra, Nehemiah

Judah Returns to the Promised Land

Talk Notes

I. Overview of Session Six: Three Periods on the Chart

II. Divided Kingdom

    A. Everything changes here

        1. Israel divides

        2. The prophets begin here

    B. 930 BC – The kingdom divides (1 Kings 12:6)

        1. Rehoboam's decision

        2. Jeroboam leads the North to separate from the house of David

        3. How to read the Chart

    C. Two kingdoms

        1. Ten tribes to the North, two to the South

        2. Israel (North)

            a. Capital: Samaria

            b. King: Jeroboam

        3. Judah (South)

            a. Capital: Jerusalem

            b. King: Rehoboam (Solomon's son)

        4. Prophets move people to obey God's Word

    D. Jeroboam's dilemma: no access to Temple

        1. A new religion

        2. Result: nine dynasties in the North (versus one in the South)

E. Keeping the kings and prophets straight

    1. Kings of Israel and Judah (see charts on pages 52 and 53)

    2. Prophets of the Northern and Southern Kingdoms (see chart on page 54)

F. Key prophets to the Northern Kingdom

    1. Amos

    2. Hosea: You have been unfaithful

G. Key prophets to the Southern Kingdom

    1. Isaiah warns of exile

    2. Jeremiah prophesies exile for seventy years

H. How to read 1 and 2 Kings

    1. Supplemental books: 1 and 2 Chronicles

III. Exile

A. The Exile on the Chart

B. Remembering the world powers: **E**at **A** **B**ig **P**urple **GR**ape

    1. Assyria: world power when Israel is exiled

    2. Babylon: world power when Judah is exiled

C. Focus on the North (Israel)

    1. 722 BC – exile by Assyria

    2. Assyria settles Samaria with captives from five other nations

D. Focus on the South (Judah)

    1. Jeremiah 34: unfaithful

    2. 587 BC – Babylon destroys Jerusalem

E. Three waves of exile to Babylon

    1. 605 BC – Daniel

    2. 597 BC – Ezekiel, Baruch

    3. 586/587 BC – destruction of Jerusalem

IV. Return: Brighter Days Ahead

A. The Return on the chart

B. Cyrus of Persia is foretold by Isaiah (Isaiah 45): allows Judah to return

C. Three "waves" of return

    1. 537 BC – Zerubbabel rebuilds the Temple

    2. 458 BC – Ezra returns and teaches the Law

    3. 444 BC – Nehemiah returns and rebuilds Jerusalem walls

D. Spiritual lessons: ingredients to rebuild your life

    1. Eucharist (worship)

    2. Word (teaching)

    3. Community

E. Ahead: a new return from exile to sin

- Takeaways -

1. God provides the Eucharist, the Word of God, and the Church to heal our brokenness.

2. There is always hope of restoration.

Discussion Questions

1. Shortly after Solomon's death, the glorious Royal Kingdom splits in two. (Look at the map on page 44. The line of division is just north of Jerusalem.) What precipitates this division? See **1 Kings 12:6-11.**

2. What are the two resulting kingdoms called?

   Northern Kingdom: _____

   Southern Kingdom: _____

3. What grave sin does King Jeroboam commit soon after the Northern Kingdom is formed? (See **1 Kings 12:26-30.**) Why does he do this?

4. **Think About It:** In what sense is Israel and Judah's punishment for their sin a physical reflection of their spiritual state?

5. The dark period of the Divided Kingdom is represented by the color black. What color is used to help recall the priod of the Exile, and why?

6. Read **Jeremiah 31:31-33.** God says that Israel has broken the covenant they made with him. Look along the top of your Chart where the covenant icons in "God's Family Plan" appear. What is this "New Covenant" Jeremiah announces? When will it be made?

7. How might looking to "other gods" in our culture result in a spiritual exile from God? Search your heart to see if you have any idolatrous attachments in your life.

8. What color is used to characterize the period of Return? Why?

9. What unlikely person does God use to return his people to the Promised Land? How is the Return accomplished? (See **Ezra 1:1-4** for help with this question.)

10. What three kinds of rebuilding are necessary when the Jews return?

Closing Prayer

God's plan unfolded through history and gives us the "story" for our lives. Let us pray in the name of Jesus.

Israel split into rival kingdoms and fell into idolatry:

R: *Help us to choose your kingdom over other loves.*

You punished first Israel and then Judah with exile. Prophets brought a message of hope:

R: *In our exile due to sin, show us the way home.*

You brought the exiles back to Canaan; they rebuilt the Temple and Jerusalem and were taught once more from your Law:

R: *Rebuild our broken hearts and lives as we return to you.*

Our Father …

Home Preparation: Looking Ahead

After a number of generations, a new foreign power comes on the scene, and the Jews are faced with a new threat. Will they succumb to a pagan culture and religion, or will they be faithful to God? The Maccabean Revolt tells this stirring story of faith and courage.

The Old Testament is finished, and the time for fulfillment of God's promises has come. God's people have been waiting for the Messiah for centuries, and the long years of spiritual exile end at last in the period of Messianic Fulfillment. Will the Jews recognize the Son of Man and the kingdom he has come to establish on earth?

- Use your Chart to fill in the following information about these time periods:

    Period name: _____*Maccabean Revolt*_____ Approximate dates: _____

    Period color: _____ Color meaning: _____

    List two main events: _____ _____

    Name the new world power: _____

    Period name: _____*Messianic Fulfillment*_____ Approximate dates: _____

    Period color: _____ Color meaning: _____

    Narrative book: _____ Supplemental books: _____

    (Note: The four Gospels are of equal importance. Luke was chosen as the narrative book for this session because it includes the infancy narrative and provides a more complete story of the history covered in The Bible Timeline *Learning System.)*

- Read the following passages to get a summary of the period of the Maccabean Revolt and some key events in Messianic Fulfillment:

    Maccabean Revolt:

    1 Maccabees 1, 2 . . . . . . Maccabean revolt

    2 Maccabees 7 . . . . Seven martyrs and their mother

    Messianic Fulfillment – Part 1:

    Luke 1–4 . . . . Announcement of the birth of the Messiah; temptation in the desert

    Luke 6:12-36 . . . . The twelve apostles; the Sermon on the Plain

    Luke 9:1-36 . . . . Sending out of the Twelve; feeding of the five thousand; Peter's confession of faith; the Transfiguration

KINGS OF ISRAEL (NORTHERN KINGDOM)
930–722 BC: NINE DYNASTIES*

No.	King	Date BC	Bad/Good	Years Reigned	Relation to Predecessor	End of Reign	Scripture Reference
1	Jeroboam I	930–909	Bad	22		Stricken by God	1 Kings 11:26–14:20
2	Nadab	909–908	Bad	2	Son	Killed by Baasha	1 Kings 15:25–28
3	Baasha	908–886	Bad	24	Son of Ahijah	Died	1 Kings 15:16–16:7
4	Elah	886–885	Bad	2	Son	Killed by Zimri	1 Kings 16:6–14
5	Zimri	885	Bad	7 days	Captain of Chariot	Suicide by Fire	1 Kings 16:9–20
6	(Tibni)**	885–880	Bad	7	Son of Ginath	Died	1 Kings 16:21–22
7	Omri	885–874	Bad	12	Captain of Army	Died	1 Kings 16:23–28
8	Ahab	874–853	Bad	22	Son	Wounded in Battle	1 Kings 16:28–22:40
9	Ahaziah	853–852	Bad	2	Son	Fell to His Death	1 Kings 22:40–2 Kings 1:18
10	Joram	852–841	Bad	12	Brother	Killed by Jehu	2 Kings 3:1–9:25
11	Jehu	841–814	Bad	28	(none)	Died	2 Kings 9:1–10:36
12	Jehoahaz	814–798	Bad	17	Son	Died	2 Kings 13:1–9
13	Jehoash	798–782	Bad	16	Son	Died	2 Kings 13:10–14:16
14	Jeroboam II	793–753	Bad	41	Son	Died	2 Kings 14:23–29
15	Zechariah	753	Bad	6 months	Son	Killed by Shallum	2 Kings 14:29–15:12
16	Shallum	752	Bad	1 month	(none)	Killed by Menahem	2 Kings 15:10–15
17	Menahem	752–742	Bad	10	(none)	Died	2 Kings 15:15–22
18	Pekahiah	742–740	Bad	2	Son	Killed by Pekah	2 Kings 15:22–26
19	Pekah	740–732	Bad	20	Captain of Army	Killed by Hoshea	2 Kings 15:27–31
20	Hoshea	732–722	Bad	9	(none)	Exile to Assyria	2 Kings 15:30–17

* Shading indicates divisions between the nine dynasties that ruled the Northern Kingdom.

** Tibni, who unsuccessfully contended with Omri for the throne after Zimri's death, does not count as a separate dynasty. His name is in the chart because his reign is mentioned in the Bible, and because he is included in some lists of kings of Israel.

KINGS OF JUDAH (SOUTHERN KINGDOM)
930–586 BC: ONE DYNASTY

No.	King	Date BC	Bad/Good	Years Reigned	Relation to Predecessor	End of Reign	Scripture Reference
1	Rehoboam I	930–913	Bad	17	Son of Solomon	Died	1 Kings 11:42–14:31
2	Abijah	913–910	Bad	3	Son	Died	1 Kings 14:31–15:8
3	Asa	910–869	Good	41	Son	Died	1 Kings 15:8–24
4	Jehoshaphat	872–848	Good	25	Son	Died	1 Kings 22:41–55
5	Jehoram	848–841	Bad	8	Son	Stricken by God	2 Kings 8:16–24
6	Ahaziah	841	Bad	1	Son	Killed by Jehu	2 Kings 8:24–9:29
7	Athaliah	841–835	Bad	7	Mother	Killed by Army	2 Kings 11:1–20
8	Joash	835–796	Good	40	Grandson	Killed by Servants	2 Kings 11:1–12:21
9	Amaziah	796–767	Good	29	Son	Killed by Court	2 Kings 14:1–20
10	Uzziah	792–740	Good	52	Son	Stricken by God	2 Kings 15:1–7
11	Jotham	750–732	Good	16	Son	Died	2 Kings 15:32–38
12	Ahaz	735–715	Bad	16	Son	Died	2 Kings 16:1–20
13	Hezekiah	715–686	Good	29	Son	Died	2 Kings 18:1–20:21
14	Manasseh	697–642	Bad	55	Son	Died	2 Kings 21:1–18
15	Amon	642–640	Bad	2	Son	Killed by Servants	2 Kings 21:19–26
16	Josiah	640–609	Good	31	Son	Wounded in Battle	2 Kings 22:1–23:30
17	Johoahaz	609	Bad	3 Months	Son	Exiled to Egypt	2 Kings 23:31–33
18	Jehoiakim	609–598	Bad	11	Brother	Died in Seige	2 Kings 23:34–24:5
19	Jehoiachin	598–597	Bad	3 Months	Son	Exiled to Babylon	2 Kings 24:6–16
20	Zedekiah	597–586	Bad	11	Uncle	Exiled to Babylon	2 Kings 24:17–25:30

PROPHETS OF THE NORTHERN AND SOUTHERN KINGDOMS
870–424 BC

No.	Prophet	Date BC	Pre/Post-Exile	Audience	World Ruler	Scripture Reference
1	Elijah	870	Pre-Exile	Israel	Assyria	1 Kings 17–2 Kings 2:15
2	Elisha	850	Pre-Exile	Israel	Assyria	1 Kings 19:1–2 Kings 13:21
3	Jonah	800–753	Pre-Exile	Assyria	Assyria	2 Kings 13:10-25, 14:23-29 *
4	Amos	760–753	Pre-Exile	Israel	Assyria	2 Kings 14:23–15:7 *
5	Hosea	750–715	Pre-Exile	Israel	Assyria	2 Kings 14:23–18:12 *
6	Isaiah	740–680	Pre-Exile	Judah	Assyria	2 Kings 15:1–20:21; 2 Chronicles 26:16–32:33 *
7	Micah	735–700	Pre-Exile	Judah	Assyria	2 Kings 15:32–19:37; 2 Chronicles 27:1–32:23 *
8	Joel	c. 722–701	Pre-Exile	Judah	Assyria	2 Kings 17–22; 2 Chronicles 29–33 *
9	Nahum	664–654	Pre-Exile	Assyria	Assyria	2 Kings 21:1-18; 2 Chronicles 33:1-20 *
10	Zephaniah	632–628	Pre-Exile	Judah	Assyria	2 Kings 22:1-2; 2 Chronicles 34:1-7 *
11	Jeremiah	625–580	Pre-Exile	Judah	Assyria/Babylon	2 Kings 22:3–25:30; 2 Chronicles 34:1–36:21 *
12	Habakkuk	610–605	Pre-Exile	Judah	Babylon	2 Kings 23:3–24:7; 2 Chronicles 36:1-8 *
13	Baruch	600	Exile	Judah	Babylon	2 Kings 24:8–25:30; 2 Chronicles 36:9-21 *
14	Daniel	605–535	Exile	Exiles	Babylon/Persia	2 Kings 23:34–25:30; 2 Chronicles 36:4-23 *
15	Ezekiel	590–571	Exile	Exiles	Babylon	2 Kings 24:8–25:30; 2 Chronicles 36:9-21 *
16	Obadiah	c. 586	Exile	Edom	Babylon	2 Kings 24:8–25:30; 2 Chronicles 36:9-21 *
17	Haggai	520	Post-Exile	Judah	Persia	Ezra 5:1–6:15 *
18	Zechariah	520–480	Post-Exile	Judah	Persia	Ezra 5:1–6:15 *
19	Malachi	432–424	Post-Exile	Judah	Persia	Ezra 5:1–6:15 *

* These prophets also have Old Testament books named after them.

MACCABEAN REVOLT

1 Maccabees

Faithful Jews Fight to Preserve Their Identity

MESSIANIC FULFILLMENT – PART 1

Luke

Christ Jesus Fulfills God's Promises

The Flight into Egypt, by Edwin Long

Talk Notes

I. Maccabean Revolt

A. The Maccabean Revolt on the Chart

B. Remembering the world powers: "**E**at **A B**ig **P**urple **GR**ape"

C. Historical background

   1. 332 BC – Alexander the Great

   2. 301 BC – The Ptolemies begin rule from Egypt

      a. Septuagint (Greek translation of Hebrew Scriptures)

      b. Tolerance

   3. 200 BC – Seleucid rule begins – enforced hellenization

D. Antiochus Epiphanes desecrates the Temple

E. Mattathias' revolt

F. Purified Temple (Hanukkah, Feast of Dedication or Lights)

G. Judas Maccabeus, a "type" of the Messiah

H. Simon Maccabeus and sons: Hasmonean rule

I. Rome rises as the new world power

II. Transition to Messianic Fulfillment

A. Developments in Judaism

B. Setting the stage: the Roman Republic

   1. Rule of Julius Caesar

   2. Octavian defeats Mark Antony

      a. Caesar Augustus: "son of God," bearer of good news for the world

    b. At this time: The real "God-man" is born in Bethlehem

III. Messianic Fulfillment – Part 1

A. The Bible is Christocentric

B. Who is Jesus?

    1. A Jew (tribe of Judah)

    2. A rabbi

    3. The promised Messiah

    4. One person, two natures ("hypostatic union")

    5. The only-begotten Son of God

C. Jesus recapitulates the "story" and fulfills it in his life

    1. Matthew 3–4

    2. Early World

        a. The first Garden, Eden; last garden, Gethsemane

        b. First and last Adam, the woman and her seed

    3. Patriarchs: Abraham will sacrifice his son; God offers his Son

    4. Egypt and Exodus: Passover lamb; God's Paschal Lamb, Jesus

    5. Desert Wanderings: Israel wanders forty years; Jesus in desert forty days

    6. Conquest and Judges: Joshua enters Canaan from Jordan; Jesus begins public ministry there

    7. Royal Kingdom: God establishes his throne through David; Jesus assumes the throne of David

    8. Divided Kingdom: Israel loses access to the Temple; Jesus becomes the new Temple

    9. Exile – Ezekiel: God himself will shepherd his sheep; Jesus is the Good Shepherd

    10. Return: Israel returns from exile; Jesus leads people back from exile and sin

11. Maccabean Revolt: Judas Maccabeus leads revolt against enemy Greece; Jesus leads final revolt against true enemy, Satan and sin

D. What Jesus has come to do (see also CCC 456–667)

1. He redeems us (John 1:29)

2. He reveals how much God loves us (John 3:16)

3. He shows us how to live (John 14:6)

4. He gives us power to become children of God (1 John 3:1; John 1:12)

5. He reconstitutes Israel around himself

   a. He is the new Moses giving the new law

   b. He chooses twelve apostles for twelve tribes

6. Jesus establishes his authority in the Church

   a. Matthew 16:13-20 – Peter as first "prime minister"

   b. *Al ha-bayit,* "over the household"

   c. Papacy: to hold the house together in the absense of the King

   d. Isaiah 22: the Old Testament "prime minister"

- Takeaways -

1. **We study the Old Testament because Jesus fulfills it.**

2. **God loves *you* so much that he sent his Son for *you*.**

Discussion Questions

1. What kind of crisis confronts the Jews at the beginning of the Maccabean period when Greece becomes the world power?

2. Based on the story of the Maccabees, what evidence do you see that Israel is learning to trust God?

3. The period of the Maccabean Revolt concludes the Old Testament story. At this point, what positive progress has been made in God's plan to restore his children to himself? Refer to God's promises to Abraham and "God's Family Plan" on *The Bible Timeline* Chart.

4. What remains to be done?

5. Open your Bible to the first book of the New Testament, the Gospel of Matthew, and read the first verse. Imagine you are a first-century Jew who knows the story. What does this verse mean to you?

6. How does Jesus fulfill the following promises of the Old Covenant in the New Covenant? *(Optional: Can you name the period and books of the Bible that describe each of these promises? Can you explain the context in which each promise was given?)*

    • The seed of the woman will crush the head of the Serpent.

    • God will provide a Lamb for the sacrifice.

    • God's people will have a land, nation, and kingdom.

    • The kingdom will be ruled by one who sits on the throne of David forever.

    • Israel will be a source of blessing for the entire world.

7. Based on Jeff's presentation, what are six things Jesus has come to do?

    1)

    2)

    3)

    4)

    5)

    6)

Closing Prayer

*God's plan unfolded through history and gives us the "story"
for our lives. Let us pray in the name of Jesus.*

Mattathias and his sons stood up against the threats of hellenization:

R: Help us resist worldliness in our culture and follow only you.

You sent your only Son, Jesus Christ, the Messiah, to fulfill all your promises:

R: Give us new life in him.

Our Father …

Home Preparation: Looking Ahead

At the close of his earthly ministry, Jesus commissions his apostles to spread the message of salvation to the ends of the earth. The seed of Abraham, bearing fruit in the Church, will now become a blessing to the world.

- Use your Chart to fill in the following information about this final period:

  Period name: _____ *The Church* _____ Approximate dates: _____

  Period color: _____ Color meaning: _____

  Name the three "waves of witness" that form the structure of this period:

  _____   _____

  _____

- Read the following passages to prepare for the periods of Messianic Fulfillment – Part 2 and The Church:

  Messianic Fulfillment – Part 2:

  Luke 22–24 . . . . The Last Supper and the passion, death, and resurrection of Jesus

  The Church:

  Acts 1:1-11. . . . . The Ascension
  Acts 2 . . . . Pentecost
  Acts 7–8 . . . . Stephen's martyrdom; the message begins to spread
  Acts 9–11 . . . . Saul's conversion; Peter's vision

Please turn the page for *Home Preparation: Review*.

Home Preparation: Review

Using your Chart or Bookmark, review the *The Bible Timeline* period colors and meanings. Have you memorized the colors yet? Complete the list that you started on page 41:

	Period Name	Color	Color Meaning	Phrase
7.				
8.				
9.				
10.				
11.				
12.				

MESSIANIC FULFILLMENT – PART 2

Luke

Christ Jesus Fulfills God's Promises

THE CHURCH

Acts

Christ's Work Continues in His Kingdom, the Church

CONTINUING THE JOURNEY

The Baton Is Passed to You

Talk Notes

I. **Messianic Fulfillment – Part 2**

    A. Passion week

        1. Last Supper

            a. Institution of the Eucharist

            b. New Testament priesthood

        2. Garden of Gethsemane

        3. Jesus is sentenced to death

        4. Crucifixion and burial

        5. Resurrection

    B. All sacrifices will cease except the *todah* ("thanksgiving") offering

        1. Eucharist = "thanksgiving"

        2. Eucharist fulfills all Old Testament offerings

    C. Jesus pays the price of the broken covenant

    D. Jesus takes the place of sinners

        1. Barabbas, "son of the father," is freed

        2. Who is Barabbas?

    E. Church of the Holy Sepulchre in Jerusalem houses Golgotha and the Tomb

    F. Jesus establishes the Great Commission (Matthew 28:18-20)

        1. Our faith consists in following Jesus (see Galatians 2:20)

        2. His mission is carried out in us: to call others back to the Father

        3. He empowers us to live the gospel

4. "As the Father has sent me … so I send you" (John 20:21)

II. The Church

   A. The Church on the Chart

   B. The focus of Acts: the body of Christ (Church) living the life of Christ

      1. **KEY:** Acts mirrors the life of Christ

         a. Chapters 1–12: Peter

         b. Chapters 13–28: Paul mirrors Peter

         c. We walk in their footsteps

   C. How is this possible?

      1. "By my spirit" (Zechariah 4:6)

      2. "I will not leave you orphans" (John 14:18, NAB)

      3. "You shall be my witnesses" (Acts 1:8)

   D. The Ascension (Acts 1)

   E. Descent of the Holy Spirit at Pentecost (Acts 2)

      1. Our day of Pentecost: confirmation (CCC 1285)

      2. Evidence of disciples' changed lives

   F. The blueprint for reading the rest of the story – three waves of witness

      1. Acts 1:1–8:3

         a. Witness in Jerusalem

         b. Pentecost

      2. Acts 8:4–12:25

         a. Witness in Judea and Samaria

    b.   Saul's conversion

  3. Acts 13:1–28:31

    a.   Witness to the ends of the earth

    b.   Paul's missionary journeys

    c.   Peter and Paul, "super apostles"

  4. Read the New Testament letters in the context of Acts

G. Conclusion of Acts

  1. Abrupt ending: Is this purposeful or not?

  2. A story without an end: You are in the story now

III. Continuing the Journey: The Baton Has Been Passed to You

A. Personal reading of the Bible

  1. Ninety-Day Reading Plan (see page 70), *The Bible Timeline Guided Journal* (see page 75)

  2. Read the supplemental books in the context of the narrative

  3. Live in your Bible! Develop intimacy with God

- Takeaways -

1. **You are called to be a disciple, not just a believer.**

2. **You have been empowered by the Holy Spirit.**

Discussion Questions

1. In describing Jesus' trial, Jeff says, "I am Barabbas" and "you are Barabbas." What does he mean by that?

2. What is the "Great Commission" Jesus gives his first disciples and us? (See **Matthew 28:18-20.**)

3. After his death and resurrection, how is Jesus able to live on in his Church?

4. **Think About It:** Based on what you know about the early days of the Church, what difference does the descent of the Holy Spirit make in the lives of the apostles?

5. How are Pentecost and the sacrament of confirmation related?

6. Name the "three waves of witness" that propel the gospel message outward from Jerusalem (see **Acts 1:8**).

7. Jeff points out that Acts is like a story without an ending. So, this story includes you. How can you live the life of Christ today?

8. Jesus calls you to be more than a believer; you are called to be a _____.
   How will you live your life differently because of that?

Closing Prayer

*God's plan unfolded through history and gives us the "story"
for our lives. Let us pray in the name of Jesus.*

You sent your only Son, Jesus Christ, the Messiah, to fulfill all your promises:

R: *Give us new life in him.*

The Church carries on your work in the world:

R: *Make us faithful ambassadors of your love.*

Our Father …

Continue the Journey

- If you want a quick review of the "story," turn to Acts 7, and read about Stephen defending his belief in Christ as the Son of God to the Sanhedrin before he was stoned and became the first Christian martyr.

- Continue to memorize the twelve time periods, and review the key people and events of each period using *The Bible Timeline* Chart as a guide.

- Start reading the story on your own. The first time through, stick to the narrative books. Later, read the supplemental books in context of their time periods and narrative books. Keep your *Bible Timeline* Chart and Bookmark in your Bible for reference.

- Use the "Ninety-Day Reading Guide" on page 70 to track your progress through the fourteen narrative books. If you read four chapters a day, you will read through the entire story in about three months.

- Once you have a good grasp of the story, read at a slower pace, and meditate on what God is saying to you in his Word. Try to make Scripture reading part of your daily routine—even if it is only for a few minutes a day.

- Consider keeping a journal as you read. Each day, record the passages you read, and write about what they mean to you. Pray first; listen while reading, and offer a response to God. *The Bible Timeline Guided Journal* can help you read through the fourteen narrative books in this way.

Blessings on you as you continue The Great Adventure!

Reading Through the Bible Historically Ninety-Day Reading Plan

---

Month #1

Early World
__ 1. Genesis 1–4
__ 2. Genesis 5–8
__ 3. Genesis 9–11

Patriarchs
__4. Genesis 12–16
__5. Genesis 17–20
__6. Genesis 21–24
__7. Genesis 25–28
__8. Genesis 29–32

__ 9. Genesis 33–36
__10. Genesis 37–40
__11. Genesis 41–45
__12. Genesis 46–50

Egypt and Exodus
__13. Exodus 1–4
__14. Exodus 5–8
__15. Exodus 9–12
__16. Exodus 13–16
__17. Exodus 17–20

__18. Exodus 21–24
__19. Exodus 25–28
__20. Exodus 29–32
__21. Exodus 33–36
__22. Exodus 37–40

Desert Wanderings
__23. Numbers 1–4
__24. Numbers 5–8
__25. Numbers 9–12
__26. Numbers 13–16

__27. Numbers 17–20
__28. Numbers 21–24
__29. Numbers 25–28
__30. Numbers 29–32
__31. Numbers 33–36

Month #2

Conquest and Judges
__32. Joshua 1–4
__33. Joshua 5–8
__34. Joshua 9–12
__35. Joshua 13–16
__36. Joshua 17–20
__37. Joshua 21–24
__38. Judges 1–4
__39. Judges 5–8
__40. Judges 9–12
__41. Judges 13–16

__42. Judges 17–21
__43. 1 Samuel 1–4
__44. 1 Samuel 5–8

Royal Kingdom
__45. 1 Samuel 9–12
__46. 1 Samuel 13–16
__47. 1 Samuel 17–20
__48. 1 Samuel 21–24
__49. 1 Samuel 25–28
__50. 1 Samuel 29–31

__51. 2 Samuel 1–4
__52. 2 Samuel 5–8
__53. 2 Samuel 9–12
__54. 2 Samuel 13–16
__55. 2 Samuel 17–20
__56. 2 Samuel 21–24
__57. 1 Kings 1–4
__58. 1 Kings 5–8
__59. 1 Kings 9–11

Month #3

Divided Kingdom
__60. 1 Kings 12–15
__61. 1 Kings 16–19
__62. 1 Kings 20–22
__63. 2 Kings 1–4
__64. 2 Kings 5–8
__65. 2 Kings 9–12
__66. 2 Kings 13–16

Exile
__67. 2 Kings 17–20
__68. 2 Kings 21–25

Return
__69. Ezra 1–5
__70. Ezra 6–10

__71. Nehemiah 1–4
__72. Nehemiah 5–8
__73. Nehemiah 9–13

Maccabean Revolt
__74. 1 Maccabees 1–4
__75. 1 Maccabees 5–8
__76. 1 Maccabees 9–12
__77. 1 Maccabees 13–16

Messianic Fulfillment
__78. Luke 1–4
__79. Luke 5–8
__80. Luke 9–12
__81. Luke 13–16
__82. Luke 17–20

__83. Luke 21–24

The Church
__84. Acts 1–4
__85. Acts 5–8
__86. Acts 9–12
__87. Acts 13–16
__88. Acts 17–20
__89. Acts 21–24
__90. Acts 25–28

NARRATIVE AND SUPPLEMENTAL BOOKS*

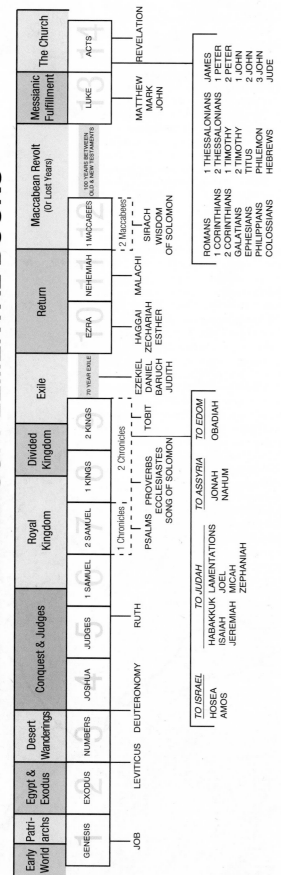

Key to Period Colors

Turquoise	The color of the earth viewed from space
Burgundy	God's blood covenant with Abraham
Red	The Red Sea
Tan	The color of the desert
Green	The green hills of Canaan
Purple	Royalty
Black	Israel's darkest period
Baby blue	Judah "singing the blues" in Babylon
Yellow	Judah returning home to brighter days
Orange	Fire in the oil lamps in the purified Temple
Gold	Gifts of the Magi
White	The spotless bride of Christ

Early World	Turquoise
Patriarchs	Burgundy
Egypt and Exodus	Red
Desert Wanderings	Tan
Conquest and Judges	Green
Royal Kingdom	Purple
Divided Kingdom	Black
Exile	Baby blue
Return	Yellow
Maccabean Revolt	Orange
Messianic Fulfillment	Gold
The Church	White

* To read Scripture in the context of the underlying narrative of God's plan, fourteen of the Bible's narrative books have been arranged chronologically in *The Bible Timeline* Learning System so that they tell the entire story from the beginning to the end. The remaining books, called "supplemental" books on *The Bible Timeline* Chart, are no less important than the narrative books but are arranged on the Chart and in this diagram in such a way that their relationship to particular time periods can be seen easily.

Outline of Bible Periods

Each numbered event corresponds to a numbered event on *The Bible Timeline* Chart.

Early World (Turquoise) Creation to 2000 BC

1. Creation . . . . .Genesis 1:1–2:24
2. Fall . . . . .Genesis 3:1-24
3. Curse and promise *(protoevangelium)* . . . . .Genesis 3:8-24
4. Flood . . . . .Genesis 6:1–9:17
5. People scattered at Babel . . . . .Genesis 11:1-9

Patriarchs (Burgundy) 2000–1700 BC

6. God calls Abram out of Ur . . . . .Genesis 12:1
7. Melchizedek blesses Abraham . . . . .Genesis 14:18-20
8. Sodom and Gomorrah . . . . .Genesis 18:16–19:38
9. Binding of Isaac . . . . .Genesis 22
10. Covenant with Abraham
    Threefold promise . . . . .Genesis 12:1-9
    First covenant (Land Promise) . . . . .Genesis 15:1-21
    Second covenant (Kingdom Promise) . . . . .Genesis 17:1-11
    Third covenant (Promise of Worldwide Blessing) . . . . .Genesis 22:1-19
11. Jacob steals blessing and flees . . . . .Genesis 27:1-46
12. Jacob wrestles with God . . . . .Genesis 32:22-31
13. Joseph sold into slavery . . . . .Genesis 37:12-36
14. Jacob's family moves to Egypt . . . . .Genesis 46

Egypt and Exodus (Red) 1700–1280 BC

15. Four hundred years of slavery . . . . .Exodus 1:1-22
16. The burning bush . . . . .Exodus 3:1–6:30
17. Ten plagues . . . . .Exodus 7:1–11:10
18. Exodus and first Passover (1280 BC) .Exodus 12:1–14:31
19. Red Sea . . . . .Exodus 13:17–15:21
20. Manna . . . . .Exodus 16
21. Covenant with Moses (Mount Sinai) .Exodus 19:1–31:18
22. Golden calf . . . . .Exodus 32:1-35
23. Levitical priesthood . . . . .Exodus 32:27-29; Numbers 3
24. Tabernacle . . . . .Exodus 25–27, 36–38

Desert Wanderings (Tan) 1280–1240 BC

25. Twelve spies sent out . . . . .Numbers 13:1-33
26. Aaron's rod . . . . .Numbers 17
27. Moses strikes the rock . . . . .Numbers 20:1-13
28. Bronze serpent . . . . .Numbers 21:4-9
29. Covenant in Moab . . . . .Deuteronomy 29:1-29

Conquest and Judges (Green) 1240–1050 BC

30. Israel crosses the Jordan . . . . .Joshua 1–4
31. Fall of Jericho . . . . .Joshua 5:13–6:27
32. Covenant renewal . . . . .Joshua 8:30-35
33. Southern campaign . . . . .Joshua 9–10
34. Northern campaign . . . . .Joshua 11
35. Tribal allotment . . . . .Joshua 13–21
36. Israel asks for a king . . . . .I Samuel 8:1-22

Royal Kingdom (Purple) 1050–930 BC

37. David kills Goliath . . . . .1 Samuel 17:1-31
38. Covenant with David . . . . .2 Samuel 7:1-29
39. Ark moved to Jerusalem . . . . .2 Samuel 6
40. First Temple built (961 BC) . . . . .1 Kings 5:1–8:66

Divided Kingdom (Black) 930–722 BC

41. The kingdom divides . . . . .1 Kings 12:16-20
42. Jezebel fights Israel . . . . .1 Kings 18–21; 2 Kings 9
43. Hosea marries a prostitute . . . . .Hosea 1–3

Exile (Baby Blue) 722–538 BC

44. Israel falls to Assyria (722 BC) . . . . .2 Kings 17:1-41
45. Foreign possession of Samaria . . . . .2 Kings 17
46. Image of the five kingdoms . . . . .Daniel 2
47. Judah falls to Babylon (587 BC) . . . . .2 Kings 25:1-30
48. First Temple destroyed (587 BC) . . . . .2 Kings 25:8-17

Return (Yellow) 538–167 BC

49. Zerubbabel rebuilds the Temple (537 BC) . . . . .Ezra 3:1–6:22
50. Ezra returns and teaches (458 BC) . . . . .Ezra 7:1–8:36
51. Esther saves her people . . . . .Esther 1:1–10:3
52. Nehemiah returns and rebuilds Jerusalem walls (444 BC) . . . . . . .Nehemiah 3:1–4:23

Maccabean Revolt (Orange) 167 BC – AD 1

53. Antiochus desecrates the Temple (167 BC) . . . . .1 Maccabees 4:43
54. Purification of the Temple (Hanukkah – 164 BC) . . . . .1 Maccabees 4:36-61

Messianic Fulfillment (Gold) AD 1–33

55. Annunciation . . . . .Luke 1:26-38
56. Baptism of Jesus (AD 29) . . . . .Luke 3:21-22
57. Sermon on the Mount . . . . .Luke 6:20-49; Matthew 5–7
58. Wedding at Cana . . . . .John 2:1-12
59. Keys to Peter . . . . .Matthew 16:13-20
60. Last Supper . . . . .Luke 22:1-38
61. Passion (AD 33) . . . . .Luke 22–23
62. Jesus gives his mother to the Church . . . . .John 19:25-27
63. Resurrection (AD 33) . . . . .Luke 24:1-12
64. Ascension . . . . .Luke 24:44-53

The Church (White) AD 33–

65. Witness in Jerusalem (AD 33–35) . . . . .Acts 1:1–8:4
   - Pentecost (AD 33) . . . . .Acts 2:1-13
   - Choosing of the seven (diaconate) . . . . .Acts 6:1-7
   - Stephen martyred . . . . .Acts 6:8–7:60
66. Witness in Judea and Samaria (AD 33–45) . . . . .Acts 8:5–13:1
   - Saul's conversion (AD 33/34) . . . . .Acts 9
   - Peter's vision . . . . .Acts 10
   - Peter's arrest and deliverance . . . . .Acts 12
67. Witness to the ends of the earth (AD 45–68) . . . . .Acts 13:1–28:31
   - Paul's three missionary journeys (AD 45–58)
      First journey . . . . .Acts 13:1–14:28
      Second journey . . . . .Acts 15:36–18:22
      Third journey . . . . .Acts 18:23–21:16
   - Council of Jerusalem (AD 49) . . . . .Acts 15
   - John's Apocalypse (AD 68) . . . . .Revelation
68. Destruction of the Jerusalem Temple (AD 70) . . . .

Continue the Journey with ...
The Great Adventure Foundational Series

Step 1
The Bible Timeline:
The Story of Salvation

Step 2
Matthew:
The King and His Kingdom

Step 3
Acts:
The Spread of the Kingdom

... and These Life-Changing *Great Adventure* Bible Studies

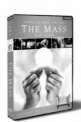

Follow Me   Mary   The Mass   Life Application

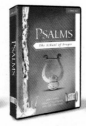

Ephesians   Exodus   Psalms   The Prophets   First Corinthians   Galatians   James   Revelation

Catholic Bible Study Resources

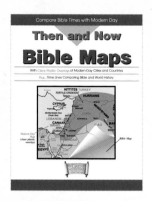

Then and Now Maps

The clear plastic overlays on these full-color maps allow you to compare the places mentioned in the Bible with modern-day cities.

20 pages - spiral bound - 8 ½ x 11

The Bible Thumper; Volumes. 1 & 2

A mini-concordance Bible verse finder with more than 1,000 easy-to-access verses to help Catholics locate and explain the basic teachings of the Faith. Each volume folds out to 33 inches and fits inside most Bibles.

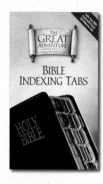

Great Adventure Catholic Bible Indexing Tabs

These pre-cut, one-inch, self-adhesive tabs fit the pages of any full-size Bible and are a great way to help you quickly locate each book of the Bible.

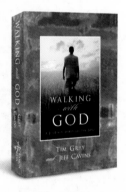

Walking With God: A Journey Through the Bible

by Tim Gray and Jeff Cavins

This captivating and inspirational book follows the central story woven throughout Scripture to reveal God's glorious plan of salvation.

296 pages

The Bible Compass: A Catholic's Guide to Navigating the Scriptures

by Edward Sri

Get the tools to study the Word of God with confidence and purpose in the appropriate context. This book demonstrates how to read the Bible within the living Tradition of the Catholic Church and addresses a host of common questions about the Bible.

174 pages

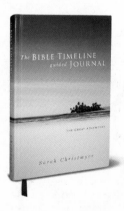

The Bible Timeline Guided Journal

by Sarah Christmyer

This is more than just a journal; it is a personal guide through the story of salvation history that will help you read the fourteen narrative books of the Bible. The journal includes room for notes as well as thought-provoking questions and tips on how to study the Bible.

236 pages

Praying Scripture for a Change: An Introduction to Lectio Divina

by Tim Gray

If you are looking for a way to get the most out of prayer, this book is indispensable. Theologian and biblical scholar Dr. Tim Gray walks you through the Bible and teaches you the simple steps of *lectio divina*, a practical and effective way to enhance your prayer life.

Book, 144 pages
Study Guide, 32 pages

Call 1-800-376-0520 or visit AscensionPress.com

Responsive Prayer

Pray this Responsive Prayer with your groups, reading up to and including the period you are studying each week, to help you learn the periods and take them to heart.

**God's plan unfolded through history and gives us the "story"
for our lives. Let us pray in the name of Jesus:
R: Speak to us as we read your Word!**

**In the Early World, you created the heavens and earth and tested Adam and Eve in the Garden:
R. Help us to always choose the life you offer.**

**In the time of the Patriarchs, you called Abraham and promised his
children land, a royal kingdom, and worldwide blessing:
R. Help us to always hope in your promises.**

**You freed your people from slavery in Egypt so they could worship you:
R. Free us from sin so we can serve and worship you.**

**You taught Israel to walk in faith through forty years wandering in the desert:
R. Help us to trust in you, O God.**

**You led Israel triumphantly into the Promised Land. They failed to teach
their children and instead did what was right in their own eyes:
R. Help us to keep our eyes on you and bring up our children in your way.**

**You established a kingdom on your servant David and promised him an eternal throne:
R. Establish your kingdom in our midst.**

**Israel split into rival kingdoms and fell into idolatry:
R. Help us to choose your kingdom over other loves.**

**You punished first Israel and then Judah with exile. Prophets brought a message of hope:
R. In our exile due to sin, show us the way home.**

**You brought the exiles back to Canaan; they rebuilt the Temple and
Jerusalem and were taught once more from your Law:
R. Rebuild our broken hearts and lives as we return to you.**

**Mattathias and his sons stood up against the threats of hellenization:
R. Help us resist worldiness in our culture and follow only you.**

**You sent your only Son, Jesus Christ, the Messiah, to fulfill all your promises:
R. Give us new life in him.**

**The Church carries on your work in the world:
R. Make us faithful ambassadors of your love.**

Our Father ...